ANIMAL CLASSIFICATION

# INSECTS

by
Charlie Ogden

KidHaven PUBLISHING

Published in 2017 by
**KidHaven Publishing, an Imprint of Greenhaven Publishing, LLC**
353 3rd Avenue
Suite 255
New York, NY 10010

© 2017 Booklife Publishing
This edition is published by arrangement with Booklife Publishing

Designer: Matt Rumbelow
Editor: Grace Jones

**Cataloging-in-Publication Data**

Names: Ogden, Charlie.
Title: Insects / Charlie Ogden.
Description: New York : KidHaven Publishing, 2017. | Series: Animal classification | Includes index.
Identifiers: ISBN 9781534520134 (pbk.) | ISBN 9781534520158 (library bound) | ISBN 9781534520141 (6 pack) | ISBN 9781534520165 (ebook)
Subjects: LCSH: Insects–Juvenile literature.
Classification: LCC QL467.2 O37 2017 | DDC 595.4'4–dc23

Printed in the United States of America

CPSIA compliance information: Batch #CW17KL: For further information contact Greenhaven Publishing LLC, New York, New York at 1-844-317-7404.

Please visit our website, www.greenhavenpublishing.com. For a free color catalog of all our high-quality books, call toll free 1-844-317-7404 or fax 1-844-317-7405.

**Photo credits**
Abbreviations: l–left, r–right, b–bottom, t–top, c–center, m–middle.

Front Cover – Doug Lemke. Back Cover – Lamyai. 2 – Lamyai. 3t – Marques. 3b – Philip Evans. 5t – paulrommer. 5m – irin-k. 6t – e X p o s e. 6bl – Mirek Kijewski. 6bm – Aleksandar Grozdanovski. 6br – Rich Carey. 7t – Guido Bohne (https://en.wikipedia.org/wiki/Deinacrida_heteracantha#/media/File:Wetapunga.jpg). 7b – Dinobass (https://commons.wikimedia.org/wiki/File:Tiny_fairy_wasp_(%E2%99%82)_on_my_finger_(7320601258).jpg). 8 – miraclebuggy. 9t – kurt_G. 9b – NokHoOkNoi. 10/11c – paulrommer. 10-11bl/tr – watin. 12t – kesipun. 12b – chaipanya. 13t – Jubal Harshaw. 13b – Deborah Lee Rossiter. 14 – arka38. 15t – Super Prin. 15b – Sebastian Janicki. 16t – Quick Shot. 16bl – MarkMirror. 16bm – SweetCrisis. 16br – Yongkiet Jitwattanatam. 17t – Dave Montreuil. 17m – D. Kucharski K. Kucharska. 17b -Apichart Meesri. 18t – Noppharat4569. 18b – Gabor Nedeczky. 19t – daraka. 19b – Dariusz Majgier. 20t – Pajjai Sapwattanapaisarn. 20b – Joseph Calev. 21tl – PhotonCatcher. 21tr – Kevin L Chesson. 21b – nattanan726. 22t – happykamill. 22b – aslysun. 23t – BHJ. 23b – tcareob72. 24 – Fer Gregory. 25t – Mikhail Kochiev. 25b – Kristof Dios. 26t – Hugh Lansdown. 26b – Dr. Morley Read. 27t – Roger Meerts. 27b – Canon Boy. 28bl – Fotos593. 28br – Dr. Morley Read. 29t – StudioSmart. 29b – Dave Massey. 30t – Chatkul. 30bl – Eric Isselee. 30br – Pajjai Sapwattanapaisarn.
Images are courtesy of Shutterstock.com, unless stated otherwise. With thanks to Getty Images, Thinkstock Photo, and iStockphoto.

# CONTENTS

Words that are <u>underlined</u> are explained in the glossary on page 31.

# THE ANIMAL KINGDOM

The animal kingdom includes more than 8 million known living <u>species</u>. They come in many different shapes and sizes, they each do weird and wonderful things, and they live all over Earth.

From the freezing Arctic waters to the hottest desert in the world, animals have <u>adapted</u> to the often extreme and diverse conditions on Earth.

Even though each and every species of animal is <u>unique</u>, they still share certain characteristics with each other. These shared characteristics are used to classify animals. There are six main groups used to classify animals. They are mammals, reptiles, birds, insects, amphibians, and fish.

This ant is an insect.

10,000 **new** species of animal are discovered **every year.**

# INSECTS

## WHAT IS AN INSECT?

Insects are part of a larger group of animals called invertebrates, which are animals that don't have skeletons or backbones. Other invertebrates include octopuses, snails, and tarantulas.

Instead of having a skeleton, most insects have an exoskeleton, which is a hard, outer shell that supports and protects the animal's body. Insects also have long antennae on their heads that they use to sense heat, movement, smells, and taste.

## INSECT CHECKLIST

- has a three-part body
- has three pairs of legs
- has <u>compound eyes</u>
- has antennae
- has an exoskeleton
- is an invertebrate

These animals are all invertebrates, but they aren't insects.

It's believed that insects make up at least half of all the living <u>organisms</u> on our planet today. We know of more than 1 million different species of insects that are alive today, but as insects are small and sometimes hard to find, people believe there are millions of species of insects yet to be discovered.

**The largest insect on Earth is a species of giant weta, known as _Deinacrida heteracantha_, and it can weigh up to 2.5 ounces (70 g)—that's twice the weight of an average light bulb. The smallest insect on the planet is the fairyfly, which has a body length of only 0.0055 inch (0.14 mm).**

Deinacrida heteracantha can only be found on one small island off the coast of New Zealand called Little Barrier Island.

fairyfly

# BODY PARTS

Even though many species of insects can look very different from one another, there are certain <u>traits</u> that all species of insects share. These traits can be used to decide whether an animal is an insect or not.

All insects have three body sections: the head, the thorax, and the abdomen. An insect's head holds compound eyes and antennae, while the thorax is where the legs and wings are located.The abdomen is the part of the body that contains the insect's <u>organs</u>.

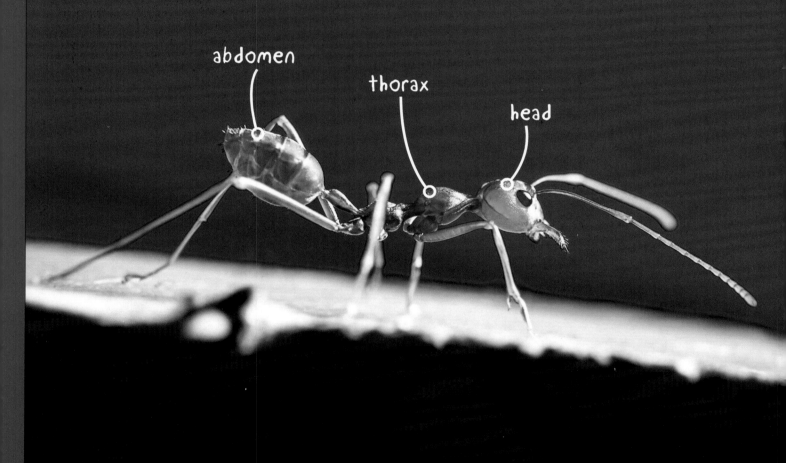

abdomen

thorax

head

Unlike many other creatures in the animal kingdom, insects don't have skeletons. Instead they have shell-like exoskeletons outside of their body. The exoskeleton helps protect and support the insect's body. As insects grow, their exoskeleton becomes too small for their body, and they <u>shed</u> it. An insect may shed its exoskeleton many times during its life, each time growing a new, bigger exoskeleton to replace the old one.

These two grasshoppers have just shed their exoskeletons.

# PARTS OF AN ANT

An ant is one of the most common insects in the world, and it has many of the traits that all insects share.

wings – Many insect species have two pairs of wings that are attached to the thorax.

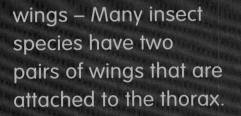

segmented body – The body of an insect is made up of three main segments: the head, the thorax, and the abdomen.

legs – All insects have three pairs of legs that are attached to the thorax.

exoskeleton – This covers, supports, and protects the insect's body.

antennae – Two long appendages are attached to an insect's head and help it feel and smell its surroundings.

compound eyes – These eyes are made out of thousands of tiny lenses. Compound eyes allow an insect to see in nearly all directions at once.

11

# GETTING AROUND

Not only do insects come in many different shapes and sizes, but they also get around in many different ways. Many insects have wings, and they get around by using their wings to fly. One insect in particular, the dragonfly, is especially good at flying and is able to hover almost perfectly still in the air.

dragonfly

cockroach

Many other insects get around by walking. Some insects, such as cockroaches, are able to climb walls and even walk across ceilings. Cockroaches can do this by using the claw-like spikes on their legs and feet, which are strong enough to grip tiny bumps and holes in the walls.

# BREATHING

Insects breathe in a unique way. They use holes in their abdomens, known as spiracles, to take air into the body. The air then moves around the insect's body through a system of tubes and sacs. <u>Oxygen</u> from the air is then exchanged with other gases in the body. This method of breathing is only good at moving very small amounts of oxygen around the body, which is why it is only done by small animals such as insects.

This is a silkworm spiracle. Spiracles allow insects to take air into their body.

It is important for every animal to breathe, or else they would not get the oxygen they need to survive.

Insects are the **only invertebrates** that are able to **fly.**

# PREDATORS
# AND ✷ PREY

All animals can be sorted into groups depending on what they eat.
The three groups are carnivores, herbivores, and omnivores.

**herbivores**
plant eaters

**carnivores**
meat eaters

**omnivores**
plant and meat eaters

Around half of all insect species are herbivores, which only eat things such as leaves, roots, seeds, and wood. This includes insects such as butterflies, ants, moths, and grasshoppers. There are also insects that are omnivores, including earwigs, which feed on fruits and leaves as well as smaller insects. Finally, some insects are carnivores, meaning they only eat other animals. One carnivorous insect is the praying mantis, which eats insects, lizards, frogs, and even other mantises!

Animals that hunt other animals are called predators, and animals that are hunted by other animals are called prey.

Insects that are herbivores aren't predators, as they don't eat other animals. Instead, most of these insects become prey for larger animals, such as frogs, lizards, and birds.

Carnivorous insects, on the other hand, are often predators. The mantis is a predator. It uses <u>camouflage</u> to help catch its prey.

Mantises are able to blend in with their environment as they wait for an animal—often another insect—to come close enough to catch. They then quickly stretch out their long, spiked front legs and grab their prey.

mantis

# FORESTS, TREES, AND LOGS

Insects can be found in many different <u>habitats</u> all over the planet. A common type of habitat that insects live in is a forest. Forests are the perfect habitat for many insects because there are many leaves and fruits for herbivorous insects to eat, as well as many safe and warm places for female insects to lay their eggs. Some insects move around the whole forest; others spend their lives in a single tree, and some even spend their entire lives in just one log.

Many species of insects lay their eggs on leaves in forests.

butterfly eggs

ladybug eggs

lacewing eggs

One insect that is able to explore a forest habitat is the butterfly. Butterflies use their large, colorful wings to fly around the forest to drink <u>nectar</u> from flowers.

A citrus swallowtail butterfly is shown here drinking nectar from a flower.

Other forest insects often stay inside a single tree. Bark beetles live, feed, and produce babies between the bark and the wood of trees.

Bark beetles are only about the size of a grain of rice.

Termites prefer to feed off dead and rotten wood.

# ADAPTATION

**Insects have adapted to their environments in many amazing ways.**

Adaptations are the different ways animals have changed over time to help them survive. Many insects have adapted to keep away predators. One such insect is the owl butterfly, which can use its wing patterns to camouflage itself as an owl. Another example is the fish-hook ant, which has hook-like appendages on its back to cause damage to any predator that may try to eat it. However, possibly the most amazing adaptation among insects is the teamwork found in insect colonies.

**The fish-hook ant has sharp appendages on its back.**

**The pattern on the owl butterfly's wings makes it look similar to an owl.**

# COLONIES

Ants help each other move food around and even make bridges for other ants to use.

When many insects from the same species all work together to find food, make a shelter, raise young, and keep away predators, they create a colony. Some insects that are well-known for living in colonies are ants, termites, and bees. Colonies can be incredibly complex—some colonies stretch over huge areas of land and have millions of individual members, each with their own specific job to do. Colonies are an amazing example of how adaptations can lead to creatures being able to work together to do incredible things.

Scientists in Brazil have uncovered an incredible system of tunnels that go 26.2 feet (8 m) into the ground. It was constructed by a giant colony of leaf-cutter ants.

# LIFE CYCLES

The life cycle of an animal is the series of changes that it goes through from the start to the end of its life.

The huge amount of <u>variation</u> between insects has led to different species often having very different life cycles. For example, some insects, such as butterflies, dragonflies, and bees, must undergo a <u>metamorphosis</u> before they can reach their adult forms. However, other species, such as woodlice and silverfish, change very little after they hatch, only shedding their exoskeletons a few times as they grow bigger.

silverfish

Woodlice shed their exoskeletons about once every two months.

# METAMORPHOSIS

There are two main types of metamorphoses: incomplete and complete.

A complete metamorphosis happens when a larva goes into a resting state, often covering itself in some sort of casing, before emerging in its adult form. Caterpillars go through complete metamorphoses before becoming butterflies. An incomplete metamorphosis happens when an insect transforms in stages, changing a small amount each time it sheds its exoskeleton.

Grasshoppers have to undergo incomplete metamorphoses before they can reach their adult form.

# LIFE CYCLE OF A BUTTERFLY

The life cycles of all butterfly species follow the same basic process.

egg

A female butterfly lays its eggs on a leaf, sticking them to the plant using a glue-like substance that the female naturally produces. After around two weeks, the eggs hatch, and butterfly larvae, called caterpillars, come out.

The caterpillar's body breaks down into a liquid inside the chrysalis. It then reforms as a butterfly, with wings, antennae, and a <u>proboscis</u>. After several weeks, the chrysalis opens, and an adult butterfly flies out. The adult butterfly will now fly to find food. It will also look for a <u>mate</u> to start the process again.

adulthood

The newly hatched caterpillar eats its eggshell and often the leaf it hatched on. The caterpillar grows quickly and needs to shed its exoskeleton, which becomes too tight for its body. It grows a new, bigger exoskeleton underneath.

caterpillar

chrysalis

The caterpillar seals itself inside a shell, called a chrysalis, that it makes out of a silk-like substance. It attaches the chrysalis to a leaf using a sticky, silk thread. After a short time, the chrysalis dries and becomes hard, providing protection for the caterpillar as it undergoes the process of metamorphosis.

# EXTREME INSECTS

Many species of insects have developed extreme abilities or unusual habits that help them to find a mate, avoid danger, or defend themselves against predators.

## FIREFLIES

Fireflies are a species of winged beetle that are famous for their amazing method of finding a mate at night. They use organs in their abdomens to give off light! The light that they give off, which is usually red, yellow or green, attracts other fireflies. Other insects are also able to give off light, but fireflies are the most famous of these insects.

Size: up to 1 inch (2.5 cm) long
Home: warm and wet areas around the world
Diet: smaller insects and <u>pollen</u>

# MAYFLIES

Size: up to 1.4 inches (3.5 cm) long

Home: all over the world in clean, freshwater habitats

Diet: algae

Molting—the shedding of exoskeletons—can be very useful for insects that undergo incomplete metamorphoses, as it helps the insects reach their adult form. While most insects that go through an incomplete metamorphosis will molt only a few times, some insects have taken molting to the extreme. Mayflies can shed their exoskeleton up to 45 times in their lifetime, sometimes leaving only a few minutes between one shedding and the next!

A mayfly is shown here shedding its exoskeleton.

Although the bullet ant has one of the strongest venoms in the animal kingdom, it's actually a very calm animal and won't attack unless it's provoked.

Some insects have developed powerful weapons to use against anything that might try to attack or eat them. One such insect is the <u>venomous</u> bullet ant, which has one of the most painful venoms in the entire animal kingdom.

These ants have developed a powerful venom to protect their colony from larger predators that might not react to a weaker venom. The sting is so painful that some have said that it feels like being shot, which is why they're called bullet ants.

Size:   up to 1 inch
        (2.5 cm) long
Home: forests and jungles
        in Central and
        South America
Diet:   nectar and
        smaller insects

# WALKING FLOWER MANTIS

Rather than develop a venom to attack other animals, some insects prefer to stay out of sight until just the right moment. The walking flower mantis is able to camouflage itself extremely well. It has adapted to be brightly colored and have large appendages that make it look exactly like a flower. Walking flower mantises use their amazing ability to blend in with flowers to stay out of sight until an insect comes close enough to grab!

Size: up to 2.4 inches (6 cm) long
Home: rain forests in Southeast Asia
Diet: insects, especially moths
        and butterflies

# INSECTS IN DANGER

Many species of insects around the world are in danger of becoming <u>extinct</u>.

One of the main problems facing many insects is deforestation, which happens when large areas of forest are cut down to collect the wood from the trees and use the land for farming. The Amazon rain forest, the largest rain forest in the world, is getting a lot smaller due to deforestation, and this has bad results for the insects that live there. Some insects only live in small areas of the Amazon, and they're in danger of having their habitat destroyed by deforestation.

Scientists have discovered 700 species of beetles on a single tree in the Amazon rain forest.

# SAVE THE BEES!

One of the most important insects to protect is the bee. Bees are pollinators, which means they help plants <u>reproduce</u>. This includes many of the plants that we get food from. Unfortunately, there are not as many bees in the world as there should be, and it's because of humans. People often spray plants with chemicals, which are known as pesticides, that kill the insects that go near them. This stops certain insects from eating the plants, but it also kills insects that don't try to eat the plants, such as bees. Unless we all make an effort to save the bees, we could find it hard to grow food in the future.

This bee has collected pollen from flowers in its two pollen baskets.

pollen baskets

# FIND OUT MORE

## BOOKS

### Insects
### by Grace Jones
(BookLife, 2017)

### Insects and Spiders
### by Steve Parker
(Gareth Stevens Publishing, 2016)

## WEBSITES

### BBC NATURE
### www.bbc.co.uk/nature/life/insect
Discover all the different species
of insects and their habitats.

### National Geographic Kids
### kids.nationalgeographic.com/animals/
### hubs/insects/
See photos, watch videos, and learn fun facts about
many different insects.

**Publisher's note to educators and parents:** Our editors have carefully reviewed these websites to ensure that they are suitable for students. Many websites change frequently, however, and we cannot guarantee that a site's future contents will continue to meet our high standards of quality and educational value. Be advised that students should be closely supervised whenever they access the Internet.

# GLOSSARY

| | |
|---|---|
| adapted | changed over time to suit an environment |
| appendages | the projecting parts that have particular functions |
| camouflage | the use of colors, shapes, or patterns that help an animal hide in its environment |
| compound eyes | eyes that are made up of thousands of tiny lenses |
| extinct | no longer existing |
| habitats | the natural homes or environments of living things |
| lenses | the parts of the eye that focus any light that passes through them |
| mate | an animal that produces babies with another animal of the same species |
| metamorphosis | the transformation that the young of some species must go through to become adults |
| nectar | a sweet liquid that plants produce to attract insects |
| organisms | any individual things that are alive, such as plants, animals, and humans |
| organs | the parts of an animal that have specific, important jobs |
| oxygen | a gas that all animals need to survive |
| pollen | a powdery material made by plants for reproduction |
| proboscis | a long, sucking mouthpart |
| reproduce | to produce new members of the same species |
| shed | to remove skin or a shell to replace it with new skin or a new shell |
| species | a group of very similar animals that are capable of producing young together |
| traits | qualities or characteristics |
| unique | unlike anything else |
| variation | differences and variety |
| venomous | able to inject poison through a bite or a sting |

# INDEX